BOSTON COMMON PRESS
Brookline, Massachusetts

1998

Boston Common Press
17 Station Street
Brookline, Massachusetts 02146

ISBN 0-936184-23-X
Library of Congress Cataloging-in-Publication Data
The Editors of *Cook's Illustrated*

How to make pasta sauces: An illustrated step-by-step guide to perfect sauces with tomatoes, herbs, vegetables, seafood, meat, and cheese/The Editors of *Cook's Illustrated*
1st ed.

Includes 45 recipes and 40 illustrations
ISBN 0-936184-23-X (hardback): $14.95
I. Cooking. I. Title
1998

Manufactured in the United States of America

Distributed by Boston Common Press, 17 Station Street, Brookline, MA 02146.

Cover and text design by Amy Klee
Recipe development by Melissa Hamilton
Series Editor: Jack Bishop

HOW TO MAKE PASTA SAUCES

An illustrated step-by-step guide to perfect
sauces with tomatoes, herbs, vegetables,
seafood, meat, and cheese.

THE COOK'S ILLUSTRATED LIBRARY

Illustrations by John Burgoyne

CONTENTS

introduction

I t has been said that the simplest things are the most difficult and this is certainly true of cooking. Recipes that require but a few fresh ingredients depend wholly on subtle aspects of preparation — how to blanch garlic to remove its bite or balancing the complementary sweet and sour flavors in tomato sauce. As American cooks, we also found that our knowledge of pasta preparation was relatively limited, more familiar perhaps with boiling buttered noodles than with the intricacies of using a mortar and pestle to prepare authentic Ligurian pesto. But once we set about careful testing of the best methods for preparing pasta sauces in an American home kitchen, much was revealed about how to combine the most authentic (and often best) methods with the practicalities of modern times. No reasonable home cook is willing to pound basil leaves for 20 minutes with a wooden pestle in a stone mortar. But a food processor does a poor job of releasing the aromatic oils in the leaves. What to do? Well, we found that pounding the leaves for just a few seconds with a meat pounder does the trick, providing most of the flavor with little of the work.

Even a simple tomato sauce can be illuminating. We found that quick cooking preserves flavor and that the type of canned tomatoes is perhaps most important, diced tomatoes being our first choice. Tomatoes packed in any sort of sauce or puree were lacking in acidity and freshness.

In addition to basic workhorse recipes, we have also added many sauces with which you may not be familiar using ingredients such as braised fennel, seared scallops, and broccoli. We hope, in addition, that this book is helpful in exploring the underlying techniques used to prepare different types of pasta sauces so that you will be skilled enough to improvise your own.

We have also published *How to Make a Pie, How to Make an American Layer Cake, How to Stir-Fry, How to Make Ice Cream, How to Make Pizza,* and *How to Make Holiday Desserts,* and many other titles in this series will soon be available. To order other books, call us at (800) 611-0759. We are also the editors and publishers of *Cook's Illustrated,* a bimonthly publication about American home cooking. For a free trial copy of *Cook's* call (800) 526-8442.

Sincerely,

Christopher P. Kimball
Publisher and Editor, *Cook's Illustrated*

chapter one

ᕗ

PASTA BASICS

OOKING PASTA SEEMS SIMPLE—AFTER ALL, who can't boil water—but there are a number of fine points that can make the difference between decent pasta dishes and great ones. Over the course of several years of writing and cooking about pasta, we have developed the following list of tips.

∷ BUY AMERICAN, IF YOU LIKE. While many sources tout the superiority of Italian pasta, our taste tests have shown this to be a myth. American brands of spaghetti scored just as well as Italian brands, and Ronzoni, which is made by Hershey Foods, topped the rankings. While

Italian brands offer a greater variety of shapes—such as ear-like orecchiette or bow tie—shaped farfalle—the quality differences that once existed between domestic and Italian pasta have disappeared.

∷ FLAVORED PASTA LOOKS BETTER THAN IT TASTES. Saffron, beet, and tomato pasta may look great, but the flavor is quite subtle. Even spinach pasta has only the mildest spinach flavor, and it's hard to detect once the noodles have been sauced. Buy flavored pastas if you like, but don't spend extra money thinking they will taste better than plain wheat pasta.

∷ USE DRIED PASTA FOR MOST RECIPES. Fresh pasta, either made at home or at a local pasta shop, is our first choice for lasagne or ravioli. It's also wonderful when cut into fettuccine and then tossed with a cream sauce (the eggs in fresh pasta work well with dairy sauces in general). However, for most uses, dried pasta, which contains just flour and water, is the best choice. Dried pasta has a sturdier texture better suited to many sauces, especially those with vegetables or other large chunks. Dried pasta is also much more convenient than fresh because it has an almost unlimited shelf-life. If you do use fresh pasta, don't buy packages from the refrigerator case in the supermarket.

These brands are soft and mushy and have none of the delicacy and subtle egg flavor of fresh pasta made at home or in a pasta shop.

▪▪ USE ENOUGH WATER. While the brand of pasta may not make much difference, how you cook the pasta does. First and foremost, start with enough water (at least four quarts for a pound of pasta). Cooking pasta in enough water is the single most important factor in preventing sticking. Pasta swells as it rehydrates and if there is not enough room, the result is a sticky mess.

▪▪ FORGET THE OIL. Some cookbooks suggest adding oil to the cooking water to keep the pasta from sticking together. We have found that abundant water will do this job. Oil will make the pasta slick and therefore less receptive to the sauce and should not be added to the cooking water. However, we do recommend using olive oil in pasta sauces. See page 43 for a discussion of buying olive oil.

▪▪ USE PLENTY OF SALT. Pasta cooked without salt is bland, no matter how salty the sauce is. Add at least 1 tablespoon once the water comes to a boil, remembering that most of the salt goes down the drain with the cooking water.

∷ TASTE TO COOK PASTA RIGHT. There are no tricks to tell when pasta is al dente, or cooked "to the tooth." (We tried throwing strands against the ceiling or refrigerator and couldn't tell when that pasta was done, but did we end up with a messy kitchen.) When properly cooked, pasta should be resilient but not chewy. Cooking times on packages or in other cookbooks are often inaccurate because each stove works differently, so tasting pasta is a must. Keep in mind that the pasta will soften a bit further once drained.

∷ DRAIN, DON'T SHAKE. Nothing is worse than a soggy, watery bowl of pasta. However, there is no need to shake the pasta bone-dry either. A little pasta water dripping from the noodles helps thin and spread the sauce. In fact, in many recipes we suggest reserving a little of the cooking water and using it as needed with oil-based sauces that may not moisten the pasta quite enough.

∷ ADD DRAINED PASTA TO SAUCE. For the best flavor and coverage, we like to add the drained pasta right to the pan with the sauce and then toss over low heat for a minute or so. This method promotes the most even coverage and also allows the pasta to actually absorb some of the sauce. Because the pasta will continue to cook in the sauce, undercook it slightly so the strands are not soft by the time they get to the table.

▪▪ RESERVE SOME OIL. For an added flavor boost, we found it helpful in our testing to save a little of the olive oil for tossing with the drained pasta and sauce. This tip is especially useful when making a simple tomato sauce. The flavor of the oil is released on contact with the hot pasta and the oil helps spread the sauce over the noodles.

▪▪ DON'T GO OVERBOARD WITH SAUCE. Italians are usually quite restrained in their use of sauces, especially because they generally eat pasta as a first course. We prefer to use slightly more sauce, but not the excessive amount common in many American restaurants. If your pasta is dry, you are not using enough sauce. If you finish the pasta and there is still sauce in the bowl, you are using too much.

▪▪ CHOOSE THE RIGHT SHAPE. In Italy there is a fine art to matching pasta shapes and sauces. However, we find that there is only one important consideration—the texture of the sauce. A very chunky sauce is better with shells or rigatoni than spaghetti because the former shapes can trap and hold pieces of the sauce, while large chunks of vegetables, for instance, would just sit on top of long, thin strands. The idea is to eat the sauce and pasta in the same mouthful. The headnote to each recipe makes some suggestions about the appropriate pasta shape. *See* also figures 1 and 2.

∷ SERVING SIZES. Every sauce recipe in this book is designed to coat one pound of pasta. For the most part, one pound of pasta will serve four as a main course. Of course, if the sauce is particularly rich, if there are kids at the table, or if there are a lot of other foods being served, you may be able to get five or six servings. As a first course in the Italian style, a pound of pasta will yield six to eight servings.

∷ USE CHEESE AS YOU LIKE. While grated cheese is a ubiquitous accompaniment to pasta in this country, not so in Italy. Italians would never serve cheese with seafood and often omit it with oil-based vegetable sauces. Of course, you can do as you like. We find that grated cheese works best when the sauce is fairly liquid, made with either cream or tomatoes. Otherwise, the cheese may stick to the pasta and make it seem dry.

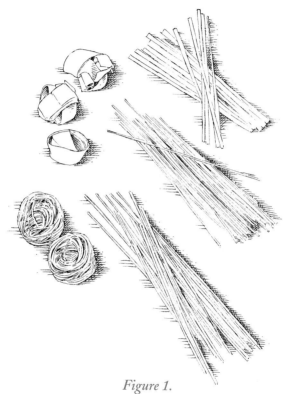

Figure 1.

Long strands are best with smooth sauces or sauces with very small chunks. In general, wider long noodles, such as pappardelle and fettuccine, can support slightly chunkier sauces than the very thin noodles. Clockwise from the top right, the shapes shown are fettuccine, linguine, spaghetti, capellini, and pappardelle.

14

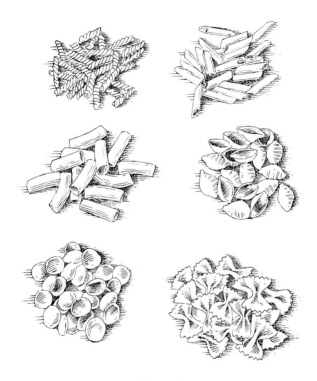

Figure 2.

Short tubular or molded pasta shapes do an excellent job of trapping chunkier sauces. Sauces with very large chunks are best with rigatoni or other large tubes. Sauces with small chunks make more sense with fusilli or penne. Clockwise from the top right, the shapes shown are penne, shells, farfalle, orecchiette, rigatoni, and fusilli.

15

chapter two

TOMATO SAUCES

HERE ARE THREE BASIC KINDS OF TOMATO sauce—a cooked sauce based on canned tomatoes, a cooked sauce based on fresh tomatoes, and a raw sauce using super-ripe summer tomatoes.

The first sauce is certainly the most useful (it can be made year-round) and also the most confusing. This basic tomato sauce should be quick to prepare and have as much fresh tomato flavor as possible. We tested dozens of variables, including the type and brand of tomatoes as well as additional ingredients, and came to these conclusions.

For the freshest tomato flavor, stick with canned diced

tomatoes, especially those made by Muir Glen, or whole tomatoes packed in juice. (We like whole tomatoes from Muir Glen as well as Progresso.) Other canned tomato products, including whole tomatoes packed in puree and crushed tomatoes, have less fresh tomato flavor because they contain cooked products such as paste and/or puree.

While diced tomatoes are our first choice, you can use whole tomatoes as long as you dice them either by hand or in a food processor. One 28-ounce can of whole tomatoes will yield about 2½ cups of diced tomatoes. Add some of the packing juice in recipes where slightly more is required.

In addition to the tomato tests, we experimented with seasonings. We found that butter mutes the flavor of the tomatoes and, for most uses, we prefer olive oil. Garlic is essential but can be overpowering. To keep garlic from burning, we puree it with a little water. A little sugar rounds out the flavors and helps balance the sweet and tart elements.

For the other two kinds of tomato sauce using fresh tomatoes, we have a number of recommendations. For cooked sauces, use plum tomatoes unless local round tomatoes are in season. With either variety, peel and seed the tomatoes before cooking them for a meaty-textured sauce. For raw tomato sauces, only local round tomatoes will do. There is no need to peel tomatoes for raw sauces, but do halve and seed the tomatoes to remove excess moisture.

Master Recipe

Simple Tomato Sauce

➤ **NOTE:** *If using whole tomatoes, avoid those packed in sauce or puree—which produces a dull, relatively flavorless sauce without the interplay of sweetness and acidity—and choose a brand packed in juice. You will need to drain the contents of a 28-ounce can and then start dicing and measuring. Depending on the brand, you may need several tablespoons of juice to yield the amount specified below. If you choose Muir Glen Diced Tomatoes, use almost the entire contents of a single 28-ounce can, without discarding any liquid. If you do not have a garlic press, mince the garlic very fine with a little salt (see figure 4) and sauté it for one minute rather than two. Serve with any pasta shape.*

2⅔	cups diced canned tomatoes
2	medium garlic cloves, peeled (*see* figure 3)
3	tablespoons extra-virgin olive oil
2	tablespoons coarsely chopped fresh basil leaves (about 8 leaves)
¼	teaspoon sugar
½	teaspoon salt

Master Instructions

1. If using diced tomatoes, go to step 2. If using whole tomatoes, drain and reserve liquid. Dice tomatoes by hand or into workbowl of food processor (use three or four ½-second pulses). Tomatoes should be coarse, with ¼-inch pieces visible. If necessary, add enough reserved liquid to tomatoes to total 2⅔ cups.

2. Process garlic through garlic press into small bowl; stir in 1 teaspoon water (*see* figure 4; if you don't own a garlic press, *see* figure 5). Heat 2 tablespoons oil and garlic in medium sauté pan over medium heat until fragrant but not brown, about 2 minutes. Stir in tomatoes; simmer until thickened slightly, about 10 minutes. Stir in basil, sugar, and salt. Adjust seasonings and serve, tossing pasta with remaining tablespoon of oil. Reserve ¼ cup pasta cooking water and use as needed to moisten sauce.

VARIATIONS:

Spicy Tomato Sauce (Arrabbiata)

Increase garlic to 4 cloves and add ¾ teaspoon dried red pepper flakes with garlic puree. Substitute ¼ cup minced fresh parsley leaves for basil.

Tomato Sauce with Anchovies and Olives

Increase garlic to 3 cloves and add ½ teaspoon dried red pepper flakes and 3 minced anchovy fillets along with garlic puree. Substitute ¼ cup minced fresh parsley leaves for basil. Add ¼ cup pitted, sliced Kalamata olives and 2 tablespoons drained capers with parsley.

Tomato Sauce with Vodka and Cream

Add ¼ teaspoon dried red pepper flakes along with garlic. Halfway through 10-minute simmering time, add ½ cup vodka. Continue with recipe, adding 1 cup heavy cream and ground black pepper to taste along with remaining seasonings. Transfer sauce to workbowl of food processor; pulse to coarse puree. Return sauce to pan; simmer over medium heat to thicken, 2 to 3 minutes.

Tomato Sauce with Bacon and Parsley

Fry 4 ounces (6 slices) bacon, cut into ½-inch pieces, in medium skillet over medium-high heat until crisp and brown, about 5 minutes. Transfer with slotted spoon to paper towel–lined plate; pour all but 2 tablespoons fat from pan. Omit 2 tablespoons olive oil from sauce and cook garlic and ½ teaspoon dried red pepper flakes in bacon fat. Substitute 2 tablespoons chopped fresh parsley leaves for basil; add reserved bacon, crumbled, along with parsley, and reduce salt to ¼ teaspoon.

Figure 3.
There are many ways to peel garlic. Unless whole cloves are needed, we crush the cloves with the side of a large chef's knife or a cleaver to loosen their skins and then peel them by hand.

Figure 4.
In a subtle tomato sauce, it's especially important to keep the
garlic from burning while still giving it time to become fragrant.
Our solution is to cut the garlic as small and evenly as possible.
A heavy-duty garlic press with sturdy handles (don't buy a cheap,
flimsy one) does this best. Mix the pressed garlic into a bowl and
stir in 1 teaspoon water to form a wet puree.

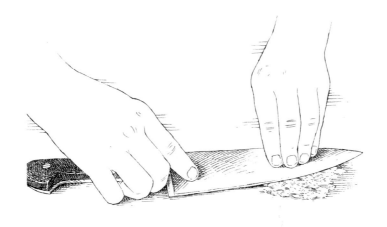

Figure 5.
If you don't own a garlic press, mince it on a cutting board,
sprinkling the garlic with a little salt and using the side of a
chef's knife to work it into a fine puree. You can prepare garlic
for all pasta sauces in this manner, if you like; it is essential
when the sauce contains just tomatoes, oil, garlic, herbs, and salt.

♔

Master Recipe

Fresh Tomato Sauce with Basil

➤ **NOTE:** *When round tomatoes are in season, use them in this recipe. Otherwise, stick with oblong plum tomatoes. The first variation is a classic in northern Italy; it has a sweet, delicate flavor well-suited to filled pastas or gnocchi, as well as any dried pasta. The second variation is a heartier sauce with strong vegetable flavor; use it with any dried pasta. We prefer to peel the tomatoes (the sauce is silkier without the skins), but you may leave them on if you like.*

2	pounds ripe fresh tomatoes
2	medium garlic cloves, peeled
3	tablespoons extra-virgin olive oil
2	tablespoons coarsely chopped fresh basil leaves (about 8 leaves)
½	teaspoon salt

♛
Master Instructions

1. Peel, core, seed, and chop tomatoes into ½-inch pieces (*see* figures 6 through 9).

2. Process garlic through garlic press into small bowl; stir in 1 teaspoon water (*see* figure 4; if you don't own a garlic press, *see* figure 5). Heat 2 tablespoons oil and garlic in medium sauté pan over medium heat until fragrant but not brown, about 2 minutes. Stir in tomatoes; simmer until thickened somewhat, about 20 minutes. Stir in basil and salt. Adjust seasonings and serve, tossing pasta with remaining tablespoon of oil. Reserve ¼ cup pasta cooking water and use as needed to moisten sauce.

▐ VARIATIONS:

Fresh Tomato Sauce with Butter and Onions

Replace oil with equal amount of unsalted butter and replace garlic with 1 small onion, minced. Sauté onion in butter until translucent, about 5 minutes, before adding tomatoes and proceeding with recipe. Omit basil.

Fresh Tomato Sauce with Aromatic Vegetables

Replace garlic with ½ cup each finely chopped onion, carrot, and celery. Sauté vegetables in oil until softened, 8 to 10 minutes, before adding tomatoes and proceeding with recipe.

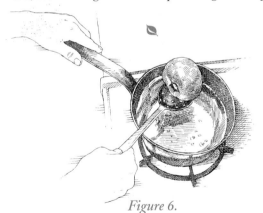

Figure 6.

To remove the skins from fresh tomatoes, drop the tomatoes into a pan of simmering water. Use a slotted spoon to turn the tomatoes (you want all sides to touch the water). After 30 seconds, use the spoon to remove the tomatoes from the water.

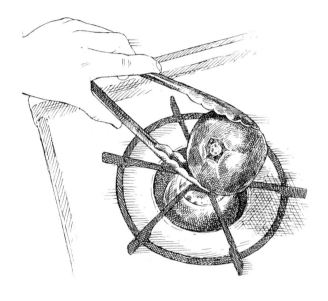

Figure 7.
If you prefer, hold a tomato with long-handled tongs over a
burner set to high. Turn the tomato often until the skin blisters
and starts to separate, about 30 seconds. This method makes sense
when peeling just one or two tomatoes, but for a whole batch you
may save time by simmering them in water.

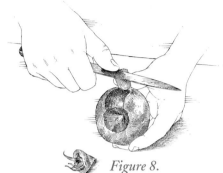

Figure 8.
With either method, wait until the tomatoes are cool enough to
handle and then cut out the core. Removing the core makes it
easy to grab hold of the skin and peel it off with your fingers.

Figure 9.
Halve each cored and peeled tomato crosswise and then squeeze
the seeds out over a bowl or into the sink. Use your finger to push
out any remaining seeds. Cut seeded tomatoes into ½-inch dice
and reserve for sauce.

♛

Master Recipe

Raw Tomato Sauce with Basil and Garlic

➤ NOTE: *Called salsa cruda in Italy, this raw sauce depends on absolutely ripe summer tomatoes. The tomatoes are seeded (but not peeled), tossed with the finest olive oil and seasonings, and then used as a sauce for pasta. If you prefer, omit the garlic. Use this sauce with penne or fusilli and serve immediately or allow the pasta to cool to room temperature (do not refrigerate) and enjoy as an Italian-style pasta salad.*

1½ pounds ripe tomatoes
¼   cup extra-virgin olive oil
1   garlic clove, minced
2   tablespoons minced fresh basil leaves
    Salt and ground black pepper

Master Instructions

1. Core and halve tomatoes crosswise. Squeeze seeds out over bowl or into sink. Use your fingers to push out any remaining seeds. Cut seeded tomatoes into ¼ -inch dice and place in bowl large enough to hold cooked pasta.

2. Add remaining ingredients, including salt and pepper to taste, and mix well. (Sauce can be covered and set aside at room temperature for several hours before using.)

Spicy Raw Tomato Sauce

Add ½ teaspoon dried red pepper flakes, or to taste.

Raw Tomato Sauce with Mixed Herbs

Increase basil to 3 tablespoons and add 3 tablespoons minced parsley and 1 tablespoon each minced mint and thyme.

Raw Tomato Sauce with Olives and Capers

Add ⅓ cup pitted, sliced Kalamata olives and 2 tablespoons drained capers.

Raw Tomato Sauce with Pesto

Replace garlic and herbs with ½ cup Classic Pesto (page 36).

Raw Tomato Sauce with Mozzarella

Toss 6 ounces fresh mozzarella packed in water, drained and shredded (*see* figure 10), with hot drained pasta and tomato sauce made with ⅓ cup extra-virgin olive oil. Smoked mozzarella may also be used in this recipe, but avoid shrink-wrapped mozzarella, which will be too dry and rubbery.

Figure 10.
Mozzarella can be shredded in a food processor fitted with
a shredding disk or by hand, using the large holes on
a standard box grater.

Figure 11.
Parsley and other fresh herbs with long stems can be kept fresh
for at least a week, if not longer, by washing and drying the
herbs, and then trimming the stem ends.

32

Figure 12.
Place the herbs in a tall, airtight container with a tight-fitting
lid. Add water up to the top of the stems, but don't cover
the leaves. Seal the container tightly and refrigerate.
The combination of water and relatively little air keeps the
herbs much fresher than other storage methods.

chapter three

PESTO AND OTHER OIL-BASED SAUCES

O LIVE OIL–BASED SAUCES ARE QUICK TO prepare and generally ready in less time than it takes to bring water to a boil and cook pasta. Their flavor is very potent, whether it's the strong punch of basil in pesto sauce or the sautéed garlic in aglio e olio.

There are a few points to remember when making pesto, the most famous of all oil-based sauces. Traditionally, this pureed sauce is made in a mortar and pestle, which yields an especially silky texture and intense basil flavor. The slow pounding of the basil leaves (it takes fifteen minutes to make pesto this way) releases their full flavor.

By comparison, blender and food processor pestos can seem dull or bland. We prefer a food processor over the blender for several reasons. Ingredients tend to bunch up near the blender blade and do not become evenly chopped. Also, to keep solids moving in a blender, it is necessary to add more oil than is really needed to make pesto.

We tested various methods for releasing more of the basil and anise notes in leaves destined for the food processor, including chopping, tearing, and bruising them. In the end, we settled on packing basil leaves in a plastic bag and bruising them with a meat pounder or rolling pin.

The other main issue with pesto is taming the acrid, overpowering garlic flavor. We tested roasting, sautéing, and infusing oil with garlic flavor, but found all these methods lacking. However, blanching tames the harsh garlic notes and loosens its skin for easy peeling.

To bring out the full flavor of the nuts, toast them in a dry skillet before processing. Almonds are relatively sweet but are fairly hard, so they give pesto a coarse, granular texture. Walnuts are softer but still fairly meaty in texture and flavor. Pine nuts yield the smoothest, creamiest pesto.

Once basic basil pesto is mastered, other variations are possible. All of these sauces should be thinned with some pasta cooking water to facilitate good distribution throughout the pasta, soften flavors, and highlight creaminess.

Classic Pesto

➤ NOTE: *Basil usually darkens in homemade pesto, but you can boost the green color by adding the optional parsley. For sharper flavor, substitute 1 tablespoon finely grated Pecorino Romano cheese for 1 tablespoon of the Parmesan. Serve with long, thin pasta or a shape, like fusilli, that can trap bits of the pesto. Pasta with pesto can be served immediately or allowed to cool and eaten at room temperature.*

¼ cup pine nuts, walnuts, or almonds

3 medium garlic cloves, threaded on a skewer

2 cups packed fresh basil leaves

2 tablespoons fresh parsley leaves (optional)

7 tablespoons extra-virgin olive oil

Pinch salt

¼ cup finely grated Parmesan cheese

INSTRUCTIONS:

1. Toast nuts in small, heavy skillet over medium heat, stirring frequently, until just golden and fragrant, 4 to 5 minutes.

2. Meanwhile, bring small saucepan of water to boil (or use boiling water for cooking pasta). Lower skewered garlic into water (*see* figure 13); boil for 45 seconds. Immediately run garlic under cold water. Remove from skewer; peel and mince.

3. Place basil and parsley in heavy-duty, quart-size, zipper-lock bag; pound with flat side of meat pounder until all leaves are bruised (*see* figure 14).

4. Place all ingredients except cheese in workbowl of food processor; process until smooth, stopping as necessary to scrape down sides of bowl. Transfer mixture to small bowl, stir in cheese, and adjust salt. (Cover surface of pesto with sheet of plastic wrap or thin film of oil and refrigerate for up to 5 days.) Thin with ¼ cup pasta cooking water before tossing with pasta. Reserve additional ¼ cup pasta cooking water and use as needed to moisten sauce.

VARIATIONS:

Mint Pesto

Replace basil with equal amount of mint leaves and omit parsley.

Arugula Pesto

Replace basil with 1 cup packed fresh arugula leaves and increase parsley to 1 cup packed. Reduce Parmesan to 2 tablespoons; add ⅓ cup ricotta cheese at same time as Parmesan.

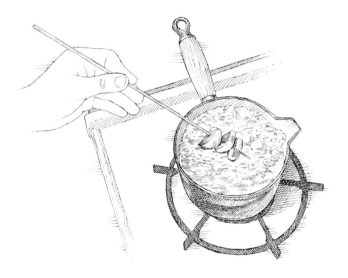

Figure 13.
Briefly blanching whole unpeeled cloves of garlic tames their flavor and prevents the garlic from overpowering the other ingredients in pesto. Skewer whole unpeeled cloves and then lower them into a small pot of boiling water (you can also use the boiling water for cooking pasta) for 45 seconds. Immediately run garlic under cold water to stop the cooking process.

Figure 14.
Bruising herb leaves in a zipper-lock plastic bag with a meat
pounder (or rolling pin) is a quick but effective substitute for
hand-pounding with a mortar and pestle and helps to release
their flavor.

Sun-Dried Tomato and Black Olive Pesto

➤ **NOTE:** *Serve with fusilli or other shape that can trap bits of the sauce.*

15	sun-dried tomatoes packed in oil, drained (about ⅔ cup)
8	large Kalamata olives, pitted
1	medium garlic clove, peeled
2	tablespoons fresh parsley leaves
1	teaspoon fresh thyme leaves
2	tablespoons extra-virgin olive oil
	Salt

⁝⁝ INSTRUCTIONS:

1. Place sun-dried tomatoes, olives, garlic, parsley, and thyme in workbowl of food processor. Pulse, scraping down sides of bowl as needed, until ingredients are coarsely chopped. Pulse in oil, one tablespoon at a time, to form smooth but still slightly coarse paste.

2. Scrape pesto into small bowl. Add salt to taste. If the olives are salty, you may need very little salt. (Cover surface of pesto with sheet of plastic wrap or thin film of oil and refrigerate for up to 5 days.) Thin with ¼ cup pasta cooking water before tossing with pasta. Reserve additional ¼ cup pasta cooking water and use as needed to moisten sauce.

Olive Oil and Garlic Sauce

➤ **NOTE:** *The key to aglio e olio (garlic and oil) is to cook the garlic slowly to tame its bite but without causing it to burn and become bitter. It's hard to make this sauce with much less oil (the pasta will be bland and dry), but the variation with lemon juice does use fewer tablespoons. Put the pasta (use either linguine or spaghetti) in the water just before starting the sauce.*

- ½   **cup extra-virgin olive oil**
- 6   **large garlic cloves, peeled**
-     **Salt and ground black pepper**
- ¼   **cup minced fresh parsley leaves**

1. Place oil, garlic, and 1½ teaspoons salt in small skillet. Turn heat to medium-low and cook, stirring often, until garlic becomes a rich, golden color, about 5 minutes. Do not let garlic brown.

2. Remove skillet from heat. Stir in parsley, and pepper to taste. Reserve ¼ cup pasta cooking water and use as needed to moisten sauce.

VARIATIONS:

Spicy Olive Oil and Garlic Sauce

Add ½ teaspoon dried red pepper flakes to oil with garlic.

Olive Oil and Garlic Sauce with Lemon

Reduce oil to ⅓ cup and add 2 tablespoons lemon juice along with parsley.

41

chapter four

౩

VEGETABLE
SAUCES

THERE ARE TWO MAIN CONSIDERATIONS when preparing vegetable sauces for pasta. First, the vegetables must be cut into small enough pieces that will not overwhelm the pasta. Broccoli must be trimmed into very small florets or mushrooms sliced. The other major issue is moisture.

Some vegetables, such as mushrooms, are fairly watery and will help create their own sauce. Other vegetables, like broccoli, need some help. Possible choices include tomatoes, cream, and oil. Tomatoes are low in fat but can obscure delicate vegetable flavors. Cream has the same problem, with additional concern about fat. Olive oil is probably the best all-purpose solution because its flavor complements that of most vegetables, but care must be taken to keep the pasta from becoming too greasy.

While it is certainly possible to use more than ½ cup of oil in a vegetable sauce meant for tossing with one pound of pasta (many traditional Italian recipes do so), we think it's better to keep the oil under ½ cup. One reason many cooks, including us, choose vegetable pasta sauces is because they make lighter, healthier meals. If you agree and want to keep oil use to a minimum, rely on a little of the pasta cooking water to moisten and stretch the sauce.

In our taste tests, we have found that pure olive oils do not have much flavor and are not recommended in pasta sauces. Extra-virgin olive oils (which contain more flavor than other olive oils and by law must have a very low acidity) are a must. In our testing, we found it quite difficult to tell differences among various extra-virgin oils when tasted on food. This held true even when comparing oils priced at $10 per quart to those retailing for $50 or more a quart.

All extra-virgin oils go through an independent tasting process that eliminates flawed samples. Our advice is to find a reasonably priced brand you like—the supermarket has many decent choices. An oil marked "extra-virgin" will deliver a certain level of quality, so you can focus on important considerations, like finding fresh, flavorful vegetables.

♛
Master Recipe

Broccoli-Anchovy Sauce

➤ NOTE: *This recipe can be made with cauliflower, broccoli rabe, kale, turnip greens, or collards. Simply adjust blanching time to insure that vegetable is cooked only until crisp-tender or slightly wilted. The hot red pepper flakes can be omitted from the master recipe or any of the variations for a milder sauce. Serve with orecchiette or shells if using broccoli or cauliflower. When made with leafy greens, this sauce works well fusilli or penne. If making the master recipe, feel free to use the anchovy-packing oil to help make up the ⅓ cup olive oil needed.*

1	medium head broccoli (about 1½ pounds)
	Salt
⅓	cup extra-virgin olive oil
4	medium garlic cloves, minced
1	2-ounce can anchovy fillets, drained and minced
½	teaspoon dried red pepper flakes

♛
Master Instructions

1. Bring several quarts of water to boil in large saucepan. Separate broccoli florets from central stalk; discard stalk and break florets into bite-sized pieces (*see* figures 15 through 17). There should be about 6 cups of florets. Add salt (to taste) and broccoli to boiling water. Cook until crisp-tender, 2 to 3 minutes. Drain and set broccoli aside.

2. Heat oil, garlic, and anchovies in medium sauté pan over medium heat until garlic is fragrant but not brown, about 2 minutes. Stir in hot red pepper flakes and then broccoli. Cook, stirring often, until broccoli is heated through, about 2 minutes. Adjust seasonings. Reserve ¼ cup pasta cooking water and use as needed to moisten sauce.

Broccoli Rabe, Garlic, Raisin, and Pine Nut Sauce

Replace broccoli with 6 cups broccoli rabe cut into 1-inch pieces and cook until tender, 1 to 2 minutes. Omit anchovies. Add ¼ cup yellow or dark raisins and 2 tablespoons pine nuts along with hot red pepper flakes and cook for 30 seconds before adding blanched broccoli rabe.

Cauliflower, Onion, and Bacon Sauce

Replace broccoli with 6 cups cauliflower florets and cook until crisp-tender, 3 to 4 minutes. Omit anchovies and hot red pepper flakes. Instead, cook 4 ounces pancetta or bacon cut into ½-inch dice in sauté pan over medium heat until crisp, about 7 minutes. Remove pancetta or bacon with slotted spoon, add enough oil to equal ⅓ cup total fat. Sauté 1 medium onion, minced, in fat until golden, about 6 minutes, adding garlic during last minute. Add blanched cauliflower and pancetta or bacon and cook until heated through. Add ¼ cup minced fresh parsley and season sparingly with salt.

Figure 15.
Some heads of broccoli have closely bunched branches that all
meet the central stalk at roughly the same point. If this is the
case, lay the broccoli on its side and use a large chef's knife to cut
the florets off about ½ inch below their heads.

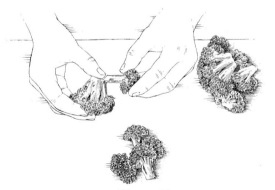

Figure 16.
Break apart florets in bite-sized pieces, snapping them apart
where individual clusters meet.

Figure 17.
If working with a head of broccoli with widely spaced branches,
place the head of broccoli upside down and use a large, sharp
knife to quickly trim off the florets close to their heads.

Escarole and White Bean Sauce

➤ NOTE: *Our panel of tasters preferred Green Giant and Goya brands of canned beans. Serve with orecchiette or small shells.*

⅓	cup extra-virgin olive oil
4	medium garlic cloves, minced
1	large head escarole (about 1 pound), trim and discard end and wilted outer leaves; cut remaining leaves into ½-inch strips and rinse thoroughly
2	teaspoons minced fresh oregano leaves Salt and ground black pepper
1	16-ounce can white cannellini beans, drained and rinsed

▓ INSTRUCTIONS:

1. Heat oil and garlic in large sauté pan over medium heat until fragrant but not brown, about 2 minutes. Add greens, increase heat to medium-high, and cook, stirring often, until greens are slightly wilted, about 3 minutes.

2. Add ¾ cup water, oregano, and salt and pepper to taste. Cover and simmer until escarole is tender, about 3 minutes. Add beans, cover, and simmer until flavors are blended, about 3 minutes. Reserve ¼ cup pasta cooking water and use as needed to moisten sauce.

Roasted Red and Yellow Pepper Sauce

➤ **NOTE:** *This room-temperature sauce works well with fusilli, penne, farfalle, or other small shapes that can trap bits of the sauce.*

2   medium red bell peppers, roasted, peeled, cored, seeded, and chopped (*see* figures 18–24)

2   medium yellow bell peppers, roasted, peeled, cored, seeded, and chopped (*see* figures 18–24)

6   tablespoons extra-virgin olive oil

1   large garlic clove, minced

2   tablespoons minced fresh mint leaves

1   tablespoon drained capers

2   teaspoons lemon juice

Salt and ground black pepper

INSTRUCTIONS:

Combine all ingredients, including salt and pepper to taste, in large bowl. Cover and set aside for flavors to meld, at least 30 minutes or up to 2 hours. Adjust seasonings. Reserve ¼ cup pasta cooking water and use as needed to moisten sauce.

Figure 18.
To prepare a bell pepper for roasting, slice ¼ inch from the top and bottom of the pepper.

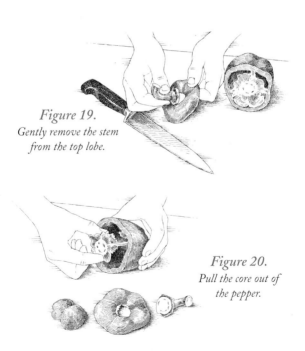

Figure 19.
Gently remove the stem from the top lobe.

Figure 20.
Pull the core out of the pepper.

51

Figure 21.

Slit down one side of the pepper, then lay it flat, skin side down, in long strips. Use a sharp knife to slide along the inside of the pepper removing all white ribs and seeds.

Figure 22.

Arrange strips of peppers and the top and bottom lobes, all pieces skin side up, on a baking sheet lined with a piece of aluminum foil. Flatten the strips with the palm of your hand.

Figure 23.

Adjust oven rack to top position and preheat broiler. If the rack is more than 3½ inches from heating element, set a jelly-roll pan, bottom side up, on a rack and then slide the baking sheet with the peppers on top of the upside down jelly-roll pan.

Figure 24.

Roast until the skin of the peppers is charred and puffed up like a balloon but the flesh is still firm. Wrap pan tightly with foil and steam peppers for 15 minutes to help loosen skins. When peppers are cool enough to handle, start peeling the skin where it has charred and bubbled the most. The skin should come off in large strips.

5 3

Braised Fennel and Kale Sauce with Balsamic Vinegar

➤ **NOTE**: *The natural sweetness of fennel makes it a good partner for bitter greens like kale, mustard, turnip, or beet. Flowering purple kale adds color as well as earthy flavor and should be used if possible. Serve with spaghetti or linguine.*

¼	cup extra-virgin olive oil
1	medium onion, minced
1	medium fennel bulb (about 1 pound), fronds removed, minced, and reserved (1 tablespoon); stems discarded; and bulb trimmed, halved, cored, and sliced thin
	Salt and ground black pepper
¾	pound kale or other bitter greens, stemmed (*see* figure 25), washed, and chopped coarse
2	tablespoons balsamic vinegar
¼	cup grated Parmesan cheese, plus more for table

⁞ INSTRUCTIONS:

1. Heat oil in large sauté pan or skillet with cover. Add onion; sauté over medium heat until softened, about 5 minutes. Stir in fennel and cook until golden, about 10 minutes.

2. Add ½ cup water and salt and pepper to taste. Stir in kale and cover. Simmer over medium-low heat until fennel is tender and greens are fully cooked, about 10 minutes.

3. Stir in vinegar and simmer to blend flavors, about 1 minute. Adjust seasonings. Toss sauce with pasta and cheese. Garnish servings with reserved minced fronds.

Figure 25.
Kale leaves have a tough central rib that must be removed and discarded before cooking. Lay the leaves curly side down, and slice along either side of the rib to remove the leafy portion.

Portobello Mushroom Ragù

➤ **NOTE:** *A ragù is a thick tomato sauce usually made with meat. Here, hearty portobello mushrooms take the place of the meat and add an earthy, woodsy flavor. Serve with penne and grated Parmesan cheese passed at the table.*

3	tablespoons extra-virgin olive oil
1	medium onion, minced
2	medium portobello mushrooms (about ½ pound), stems discarded; caps halved and cut crosswise into ¼-inch strips (*see* figures 26 and 27)
1	teaspoon minced fresh rosemary leaves
	Salt and freshly ground black pepper
½	cup dry red wine
1½	cups drained canned whole tomatoes, chopped

⸬ INSTRUCTIONS:

1. Heat oil in large skillet. Add onion and sauté over medium heat until translucent, about 5 minutes. Add mushrooms and cook, stirring occasionally, until quite tender and starting to shed their liquid, about 5 minutes. Stir in rosemary and salt and pepper to taste, and cook for 30 seconds.

2. Add wine and simmer until it reduces by half, about 3 minutes. Add tomatoes and simmer until sauce thickens considerably, 10 to 15 minutes. Adjust seasonings.

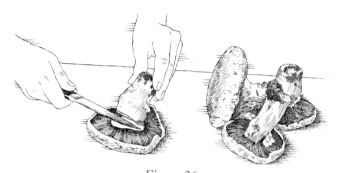

Figure 26.
The stems on portobello mushrooms are tough and woody. They can be used in stock but will remain hard if used in a pasta sauce. Simply slice them off just under the cap and reserve for another use or discard.

Figure 27.
Slice each cap in half and then cut each half crosswise into 1/4-inch-thick strips.

chapter five

ᕆ

MEAT SAUCES

BY DEFINITION, MEAT SAUCES ARE RICH IN FLAVOR and offer an excellent way to "stretch" a small amount of beef or pork to feed four or more people. Because the meat must marry with the pasta, it needs to be quite small. Ground meats, bulk sausage (or sausage meat removed from its casings and crumbled), and chopped bacon are all possible choices.

When making sauces with ground beef, we opt for chuck, which has more fat than ground round and sirloin. In our testing, we have found that leaner ground meats become dry and tough when cooked through, as is necessary when making a pasta sauce. Even chuck can lose too much moisture if it is overcooked. For this reason, sauté ground meat (as well as sausage) just until it loses its raw color. This way the meat will still retain some of its moisture when the liquid ingredients (wine, tomatoes, etc.) are added to the pan. The meat will continue to cook, so there's no need to worry about undercooking at this point.

In addition to not overcooking the meat, try to break apart pieces with a fork as the meat cooks. Ground meat, especially, has a tendency to clump together as it cooks. Pieces of meat crumbled into small bits will coat pasta better than large pieces, so don't omit this step.

Sauces in this chapter require several different kinds of canned tomatoes. For ragù, we like to use whole tomatoes in juice. We drain and chop the tomatoes and then use the juices to keep the sauce from scorching. The three-hour simmering time for this sauce accentuates differences in pans and stoves. The tomato juice, which can be added as needed, helps compensate for those differences.

For the absolutely quickest meat sauce, we use canned crushed tomatoes, which need very little time to thicken into a saucy consistency. While some chunkiness is desired in a basic tomato sauce, for meatballs the sauce should be thick (so the meatballs don't become soggy) and smooth. Canned crushed tomatoes are essential here.

Bolognese Sauce

➤ NOTE: *Italy's most famous meat sauce hails from Bologna and is called a ragù. While many recipes use a variety of ground meats, pancetta, prosciutto, and/or mushrooms, we prefer the simple, intense flavors of beef and tomatoes, fortified with wine, milk, and aromatic vegetables. Ground beef is first sautéed with onions, carrots, and celery until no longer pink. Wine is added to give the sauce depth. Once the wine cooks off, the beef is simmered in a little milk, which adds sweetness and keeps the meat soft during the final long simmering in tomatoes. Serve with fresh pasta, especially fettuccine or cheese ravioli, and pass grated Parmesan cheese at the table.*

2	tablespoons unsalted butter
2	tablespoons olive oil
1	small onion, minced
1	small carrot, peeled and minced
½	celery stalk, minced
¾	pound ground beef, preferably chuck
	Salt
1	cup dry white wine
1	cup milk
	Pinch freshly grated nutmeg
1	28-ounce can whole tomatoes packed in juice, chopped fine, with juice reserved

INSTRUCTIONS:

1. Heat butter and oil in casserole or large, deep sauté pan with thick, heavy bottom. Add onion, carrot, and celery and sauté over medium heat until softened, about 7 minutes.

2. Add beef and crumble with fork to break apart (*see* figure 28). Sprinkle with 1 teaspoon salt and cook, stirring often, until meat just loses raw color, about 3 minutes. Add wine and simmer until alcohol cooks off, about 4 minutes. Add milk and nutmeg. Simmer until milk thickens a bit, about 4 minutes.

3. Add tomatoes and ½ cup of their juice. When sauce starts to boil, reduce heat so that it cooks at barest simmer, with just an occasional bubble or two. Cook, uncovered, for 3 hours, turning down heat if sauce starts to simmer or scorch. If sauce dries out before it is done, add some reserved tomato juice. Adjust seasonings and serve. (Sauce can be stored in airtight container and refrigerated for several days or frozen for several months. Warm over low heat before using.)

Quick Meat Sauce

➤ **NOTE:** *A traditional meat sauce must simmer for three hours to acquire its characteristic depth of flavor. In this 20-minute recipe, mushrooms lend some bulk and flavor to a quickly simmered sauce. Serve with fettuccine, filled pastas (tortellini or ravioli), or even fusilli, and pass grated Parmesan or Pecorino Romano cheese at the table.*

1	tablespoon olive oil
¾	pound ground beef, preferably chuck
	Salt and ground black pepper
½	pound button or cremini mushrooms, ends trimmed and sliced thin
2	medium garlic cloves, minced
1	teaspoon minced fresh oregano leaves or ½ teaspoon dried
½	cup dry red wine
2½	cups crushed tomatoes

INSTRUCTIONS:

1. Heat oil in large skillet. Add beef and crumble with fork to break meat apart. Cook, stirring often, over medium heat until meat just loses raw color, about 3 minutes. Season with salt and pepper to taste. If there is a lot of fat in pan, carefully drain some off.

2. Add mushrooms and cook until tender, about 3 minutes. Add garlic and oregano and cook for 1 minute. Add wine; simmer until alcohol cooks off, about 2 minutes.

3. Add tomatoes and simmer until sauce thickens, about 10 minutes. Adjust seasonings and serve.

⠏⠏ VARIATIONS:

Sausage-Mushroom Sauce with Tomatoes

Replace beef with equal amount of Italian link sweet (or hot) sausage, removed from casings. Cook, crumbling sausage with fork, until pink color is gone, about 4 minutes. Add salt sparingly and proceed with recipe.

Figure 28.

Ragù must have a very fine, almost smooth texture. For this reason, it's imperative that you crumble the ground beef with a fork as it cooks. Otherwise, it may clump together into large pieces that might overwhelm delicate pasta shapes.

63

Meatballs in Smooth Tomato Sauce

➤ **NOTE:** *We found that a combination of beef and pork delivers the best flavor. The pork adds an extra dimension to the meatballs but all chuck may be used if you prefer. As for binders, we found that fresh sliced bread, with the crusts trimmed, creates moister, richer, creamier meatballs than dried bread crumbs. Buttermilk adds a subtle tang and is our preferred liquid to soften the torn bread.*

To dress spaghetti or other long, thin shape, ladle several large spoonfuls of tomato sauce (without meatballs) over spaghetti and toss until noodles are well coated. Divide pasta among individual bowls and top each with a little more tomato sauce and several meatballs. Serve immediately with grated cheese passed separately.

Meatballs

2	slices white sandwich bread (crusts discarded), torn into small pieces
½	cup buttermilk or 6 tablespoons plain yogurt thinned with 2 tablespoons sweet milk
1	pound ground meat (preferably ¾ pound ground chuck and ¼ pound ground pork)
¼	cup freshly grated Parmesan cheese
2	tablespoons finely minced fresh parsley leaves
1	large egg yolk
1	teaspoon finely minced garlic
¾	teaspoon salt
	Ground black pepper
	About 1¼ cups vegetable oil for pan-frying

Smooth Tomato Sauce

2	tablespoons extra-virgin olive oil
1	teaspoon minced garlic
1	28-ounce can crushed tomatoes
1	tablespoon minced fresh basil leaves
	Salt and ground black pepper

:: INSTRUCTIONS:

1. Combine bread and buttermilk in small bowl, mashing occasionally with fork, until smooth paste forms, about 10 minutes.

2. Meanwhile, place ground meat, cheese, parsley, egg yolk, garlic, salt, and pepper to taste in medium bowl. Add bread-milk mixture and combine until evenly mixed (*see* figure 29). Shape 3 tablespoons of mixture into 1½-inch round meatball. (When forming meatballs use a fairly light touch. If you compact the meatballs too much, they can become dense and hard.) You should be able to form about 14 meatballs. (Meatballs may be placed on large plate, covered loosely with plastic wrap, and refrigerated for several hours.)

3. Pour vegetable oil into 10- or 11-inch sauté pan to depth of ¼ inch. Turn flame to medium-high heat. After several minutes, test oil with edge of meatball. When oil sizzles, add meatballs in single layer. Fry, turning several times, until nicely browned on all sides, about 10 minutes (*see* figure 30). Regulate heat as needed to keep oil sizzling but not smoking. Transfer browned meatballs to plate lined with paper towels and set aside.

4. Discard oil in pan but leave behind any browned bits. Add olive oil for tomato sauce along with garlic and sauté, scraping up any browned bits, just until garlic is golden, about 30 seconds. Add tomatoes, bring to boil, and simmer gently until sauce thickens, about 10 minutes. Stir in basil and salt and pepper to taste. Add meatballs and simmer, turning them occasionally, until heated through, about 5 minutes. Adjust seasonings and serve.

Figure 29.
Once all the ingredients for the meatballs are in the bowl, mix with a fork to roughly combine. At this point, use your hands to make sure that the flavorings are evenly distributed throughout the mixture.

Figure 30.
*Meatballs must be browned well on all sides. This may involve
standing meatballs on their sides near the end of the cooking
process. If necessary, lean them up against each other to get the
final sides browned.*

67

Carbonara Sauce

➤ **NOTE:** *With bacon, eggs, and cheese, this sauce, which should be served with spaghetti, is an indulgence. Pancetta, Italian bacon that is cured but not smoked, is more authentic, but regular smoked American bacon is fine as well. For a sharper cheese flavor, replace ¼ cup of the Parmesan with an equal amount of grated Pecorino Romano. We found that white wine, which is common to some carbonara recipes, helps cut the richness of the sauce. Note that although the heat from the pasta will slightly cook the eggs, it will not raise the temperature sufficiently to kill bacteria and this dish should be avoided by anyone who does not want to eat raw eggs.*

2	tablespoons extra-virgin olive oil
3	large garlic cloves, lightly crushed
⅓	pound pancetta or bacon, cut into ¼ -inch dice (*see* figure 31)
¼	cup dry white wine
4	large eggs
½	cup grated Parmesan cheese, plus more for table
2	tablespoons minced fresh parsley leaves
	Ground black pepper to taste

INSTRUCTIONS:

1. Heat oil in large skillet. Add garlic and cook over medium heat, turning several times, until rich golden color, about 5 minutes. Remove and discard garlic.

2. Add pancetta to skillet and cook, stirring occasionally, until crisp, about 7 minutes. Drain off all but 2 tablespoons of fat. Add wine and simmer for 2 minutes. Turn off heat and set pan aside. Reheat bacon mixture just before tossing with pasta.

3. Meanwhile, in bowl large enough to hold cooked pasta, beat eggs, cheese, parsley, and generous amount of black pepper. Toss cooked and drained pasta in bowl with eggs. Mix well and then stir in hot bacon mixture. Serve immediately.

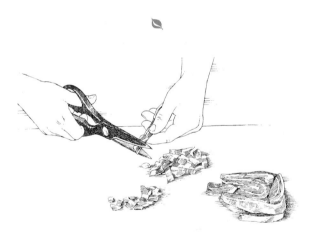

Figure 31.
Cutting pancetta or bacon can be difficult because the pieces often stick to a knife. Try using kitchen scissors instead.

chapter six

SEAFOOD
SAUCES

THERE ARE SEVERAL IMPORTANT POINTS to consider when making pasta sauces from seafood. First, most seafood will overcook quickly, so timing is essential. While a meat sauce can often simmer on the back burner for quite some time, a clam sauce can go from delicious to inedible in a matter of minutes. For the most part, this means starting seafood sauces at the same time the pasta goes into the boiling water. If the sauce is ready before the pasta, turn off the heat and cover the pan. Do not simmer seafood sauces over low heat. The heat from the drained pasta will warm seafood sauces if necessary.

The second important issue is moisture. Shrimp,

scallops, mussels, and clams are unappetizing if too dry and will not coat pasta properly. In the case of clams and mussels, the natural juices make the ideal medium for a sauce. Shrimp and scallops will need a fair amount of olive oil, wine, cream, or tomatoes to keep them saucy. Reserving some of the pasta cooking water is also a good idea.

When serving seafood pasta sauces, Italians do not pass grated cheese at the table. The Italians feel that the rich, buttery flavor of cheese clashes with the bright, briny flavor of seafood.

For the most part, we agree with the Italian sentiment. If you would like to add something to seafood pastas at the table, try toasted bread crumbs. They add a pleasing crunch and nutty flavor. Any time you have some stale bread on hand, turn it into crumbs (either by hand or in a food processor) and then freeze the crumbs in an airtight container. When needed, simply toast the crumbs in a dry skillet for an instant flavor boost for seafood pasta.

Some cleaning tips for seafood. Clams and mussels need to be scrubbed with a stiff brush to remove any caked-on mud or sand. Also, pull out any weedy "beards" protruding from the mussels. Scallops have a small, rough-texture, crescent-shaped muscle that attaches the scallop to the shell. This tendon on the side of the scallop can toughen when cooked and should be peeled off when preparing scallops.

Fresh Clam Sauce

➤ NOTE: *Large quahog clams, though they do not make great eating, provide plenty of liquid for a briny, brothy pasta sauce. And because quahogs, also called chowder clams, are so cheap, discard them without guilt and dine on the sweet, tender littlenecks with the pasta. To keep the littlenecks from becoming tough, cook them just until they begin to open in a little wine and then add them back to the sauce just before it is tossed with either spaghetti or linguine. The diced plum tomato in this recipe provides some acidity as well as color. Start the pasta at the same time you start cooking the garlic and undercook the pasta slightly, because it will be cooked again with the sauce. See figure 32 for information on cleaning clams.*

24	small littleneck clams, scrubbed thoroughly
6	large quahog or chowder clams, scrubbed thoroughly
½	cup dry white wine Pinch cayenne
¼	cup extra-virgin olive oil
2	medium garlic cloves, minced (about 1 tablespoon)
1	large or 2 small plum tomatoes, peeled, cored, seeded, and minced (*see* figures 6–9)
¾	cup chopped fresh parsley leaves

⠿ INSTRUCTIONS:

1. Bring clams, wine, and cayenne to boil in deep, 10- to 12-inch covered skillet over high heat. Boil, shaking pan occasionally, until littlenecks begin to open, 3 to 5 minutes. Transfer littlenecks with slotted spoon to bowl; set aside. Recover pan and continue cooking quahogs until their liquid is released, about 5 minutes more. Discard quahogs and strain liquid in pan through paper towel–lined sieve into large measuring cup (*see* figure 33). Add enough water to make 1 cup; set aside.

2. Wipe out skillet with paper towel and heat oil and garlic in empty skillet over medium heat until garlic starts to sizzle, about 1 minute. Adjust heat to low; cook, stirring occasionally, until garlic turns pale gold, about 5 minutes more. Add tomatoes, raise heat to high, and sauté until incorporated, about 2 minutes. Add littlenecks and cover; cook until all clams are open, 1 to 2 minutes more.

3. Add cooked, drained pasta, reserved clam liquid, and parsley and cook, stirring often, until pasta is melded with sauce, about 30 seconds. Serve immediately.

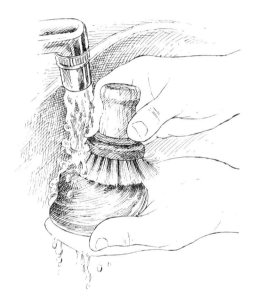

Figure 32.
Scrub clams with soft brush under running water to remove any
sand from their shells.

Figure 33.
To remove any grit from the clam cooking liquid, strain it
through a sieve lined with a single layer of paper towel and set
over a measuring cup. If desired, moisten the towel first so that it
does not absorb any precious clam juices.

Steamed Mussel Sauce with Lemon and White Wine

➤ **NOTE:** *Mussels can sometimes be gritty. To remove any sand, the mussels are steamed in white wine and the broth is strained through paper towels. The mussels and their strained liquid are added to the finished sauce just before it is tossed with the pasta. Use linguine or spaghetti and start cooking it once mussels have been steamed and the broth has been strained. This sauce is fairly soupy, so serve with bread.*

3	dozen black mussels, rinsed thoroughly and weedy beards removed (*see* figure 34)
½	cup dry white wine
¼	cup extra-virgin olive oil
2	medium garlic cloves, minced
½	teaspoon dried red pepper flakes
½	teaspoon grated zest and 2 tablespoons juice from 1 medium lemon
2	tablespoons minced fresh parsley leaves
	Salt

INSTRUCTIONS:

1. Bring mussels and wine to boil in large soup kettle over medium-high heat. Lower heat to steam mussels until most have opened, 4 to 5 minutes. Discard any that have not opened. Remove mussels from shells if desired; set aside.

76

Strain liquid through paper–towel lined sieve and reserve. Wipe out soup kettle with another paper towel.

2. Heat oil over medium heat in now-empty soup kettle. Add garlic and pepper flakes; sauté until garlic is golden, about 1 minute. Add strained mussel broth, and lemon zest and juice; simmer to blend flavors, 3 to 4 minutes. Return mussels to kettle; heat to warm through. Stir in parsley and salt to taste. Use immediately.

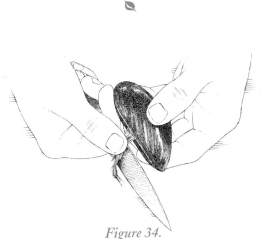

Figure 34.

Some mussels contain a weedy beard protruding from the crack between the two shells. Trap the beard between the side of a small knife and your thumb and pull to remove it.

Shrimp Sauce with Basil

➤ NOTE: *This sauce is really nothing more than sautéed shrimp tossed with pesto minus the cheese. The linguine or other long, thin pasta should be in the water when you start cooking the shrimp.*

¾   cup packed fresh basil leaves

1   small garlic clove, minced

1   tablespoon pine nuts

6   tablespoons extra-virgin olive oil
     Salt and ground black pepper

1   pound small shrimp, peeled and deveined
     if desired

INSTRUCTIONS:

1. Place basil, garlic, nuts, and 4 tablespoons oil in work-bowl of food processor; process until smooth, stopping as necessary to scrape down sides of bowl. Transfer mixture to bowl large enough to hold cooked pasta. Stir in ½ teaspoon salt and ¼ teaspoon pepper.

2. Heat remaining 2 tablespoons oil in large skillet. Add shrimp; sauté over medium-high heat until pink, 3 to 4 minutes. Season with salt and pepper to taste. Transfer shrimp to bowl with pesto. Thin with ¼ cup pasta cooking water before tossing with pasta. Reserve additional ¼ cup pasta cooking water and use as needed to moisten sauce.

Seared Scallop Sauce with Wine and Cream

➤ NOTE: *The only tricky part of this recipe is ensuring that the pasta and sauce are done at the same time. Start spaghetti or other long, thin pasta after adding the ginger and shallot to the sauté pan and you'll be fine.*

1½	pounds sea scallops, tendons discarded
	Salt and ground black pepper
1½	tablespoons unsalted butter
1	medium shallot, minced
1	tablespoon minced fresh gingerroot
⅔	cup dry white wine
2	tablespoons white wine vinegar
1	cup heavy cream
¼	cup snipped fresh chives or ½ cup chopped scallion greens

⊞ INSTRUCTIONS:

1. Preheat oven to 200 degrees. Sprinkle scallops on both sides with salt and pepper. Heat large sauté pan over medium-high heat. Add half butter; swirl to coat pan bottom. Continue to heat until butter turns golden brown. Add half of scallops, one at a time, flat side down; cook, adjusting heat as necessary to prevent fat from burning, until scallops are well browned, 1½ to 2 minutes. Using tongs (*see* figure 35), turn scallops one at a time; cook until sides are firmed up and all but middle third of scallop is opaque, 30 seconds to 1½ minutes longer, depending on size. Transfer scallops to platter and place in warm oven. Repeat cooking process with remaining butter and scallops.

2. Add shallot and ginger to empty pan; cook until shallot softens, 1 to 2 minutes. Increase heat to high; add wine and vinegar and boil, scraping pan bottom with wooden spoon to loosen caramelized bits, until liquid reduces to glaze, 4 to 5 minutes. Add cream, ½ teaspoon salt, ¼ teaspoon pepper; bring to boil. Reduce heat; simmer until cream reduces slightly, about 1 minute. Stir in chives. Toss with pasta, divide among bowls, and arrange some scallops over each portion.

Figure 35.
When sautéing scallops, make sure not to overcrowd
the pan or they will not brown properly. Use tongs to turn
the scallops in the pan.

Scallop Sauce with Toasted Bread Crumbs

➤ **NOTE:** *In this sauce, toasted bread crumbs take the place of grated cheese (which is not served with seafood sauces in Italy) and are tossed with the pasta and scallop sauce just before serving. Use linguine or spaghetti here and do not shake the pasta dry when draining. If the pasta is still coated with a little cooking water (but not dripping) it will marry better with the oil-based sauce. Start cooking the pasta just before heating the oil in step 2.*

½   cup fresh bread crumbs (*see* figures 36–38)
½   cup extra-virgin olive oil
      Salt
 2   medium cloves garlic, minced
½   teaspoon hot red pepper flakes or to taste
 1   pound scallops, tendons discarded and cut into
      ½ -inch pieces
¼   cup minced fresh parsley leaves

INSTRUCTIONS:

1. Adjust oven rack to center-low position and preheat oven to 325 degrees. Mix crumbs with 1 tablespoon oil and pinch salt to coat evenly. Spread in single layer on small baking sheet. Bake crumbs, stirring once after 5 minutes, until golden brown, about 12 minutes. Set crumbs aside.

2. Heat remaining oil in very large skillet. Add garlic and sauté over medium heat until golden, about 1 minute. Add hot red pepper flakes and salt to taste and continue cooking for another 30 seconds.

3. Increase heat to high. Add scallops and sauté, stirring occasionally, until opaque, about 3 minutes. Stir in parsley and adjust seasonings. Immediately toss sauce with pasta and toasted bread crumbs and serve.

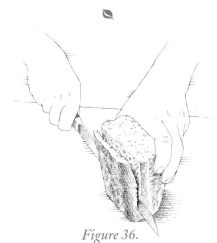

Figure 36.

To make bread crumbs, start with a piece of 2- or 3-day old country white bread or baguette. To make crumbs by hand, slice off and discard the tough and often overbaked bottom crust.

Figure 37.
Slice the bread into ⅜-inch-thick pieces. Cut these slices into
⅜-inch strips, and then cut these into cubes and chop until you
have small pieces about the size of a lemon seed.

84

Figure 38.
To make the crumbs in a food processor, cut the trimmed loaf into
1½-inch cubes and then pulse the cubes in a food processor to the
desired crumb size.

85

chapter seven

DAIRY SAUCES

AUCES BASED ON BUTTER, CREAM, AND CHEESE deliver tremendous flavor, usually with a minimum of work. It's hard to imagine a simpler sauce than butter cooked until golden brown and infused with fresh sage leaves.

There are a few rules to remember. Use unsalted butter. Many manufacturers add salt to butter to prolong its freshness. Lost in the process is the sweet, creamy dairy flavor of farm-fresh butter. Sweet (or unsalted) butter tastes better.

When buying heavy cream, try to select a brand that has not been ultrapasteurized. This process exposes the cream to very high temperatures in order to prolong shelf-life. In the process, the cream loses some freshness and takes on a cooked flavor. Regular pasteurized cream, which may be available in supermarkets and is almost always sold in natural foods stores, has a sweeter, fresher flavor.

Finally, high-quality cheeses will always make a difference in pasta sauces, even when it's just a little grated Parmesan sprinkled on at the table. When shopping for ricotta, this means avoiding supermarket varieties, which tend to be watery and bland, and going to an Italian market, a cheese shop, or gourmet store and getting fresh homestyle ricotta that is firmer, creamier, and drier (it should have a texture like goat cheese) and much more flavorful.

Some tips for buying and grating Parmesan cheese: The real thing, Parmigiano-Reggiano, will deliver the best results. Look for these words stenciled on the rind. In our tests, we found that cheese grated directly over pasta has the fullest flavor. However, you can grate cheese before dinner and place some in a bowl on the table. If you have extra, it can be stored in the refrigerator. In our tests, grated cheese lost some flavor after a week, but the quality did not become significantly worse than freshly grated cheese until a month in the refrigerator. At this point, the grated cheese was quite dry and a bit bitter. Our advice: Grate cheese as needed but feel free to refrigerate extra in an airtight container and use it within a week or so.

Butter and Sage Sauce

➤ **NOTE:** *This is the simplest of all sauces. It is especially good with filled fresh pasta like ravioli and tortellini. It also works with fresh fettuccine or any dried pasta. Serve with grated Parmesan cheese at the table.*

8 **tablespoons unsalted butter**
2 **tablespoons minced fresh sage leaves**
   Salt

INSTRUCTIONS:

Place butter, sage, and ½ teaspoon salt in medium skillet set over medium heat. Cook, swirling pan occasionally, until butter is golden brown, about 5 minutes. Use immediately.

VARIATION:

Butter and Pine Nut Sauce

Toast 2 tablespoons chopped pine nuts in medium skillet over medium heat until golden and fragrant, about 5 minutes. Set nuts aside, then proceed with recipe, omitting sage and adding toasted nuts and 2 tablespoons minced fresh parsley leaves when butter has turned golden brown.

88

Alfredo Sauce

➤ **NOTE:** *With butter, cream, and cheese, this sauce is certainly a luxury. However, when paired with fresh fettuccine, the results are incomparable. Start cooking dried pasta before starting the sauce; fresh pasta can be added to the boiling water at the same time the cream and butter are heating. Undercook the pasta slightly; it finishes cooking in the cream sauce.*

1	cup heavy cream
3	tablespoons unsalted butter
⅔	cup grated Parmesan cheese, plus more for table
	Salt and ground black pepper
	Grated fresh nutmeg

INSTRUCTIONS:

1. Place ⅔ cup cream and butter over medium heat in sauté pan large enough to hold cooked pasta. Bring to boil; simmer until thickened, about 30 seconds.

2. Add cooked, drained pasta to cream sauce, tossing to coat noodles. Add remaining cream, cheese, salt and pepper to taste, and nutmeg. Continue tossing until cream thickens a bit and pasta is nicely coated, about 30 seconds. Adjust seasonings and serve immediately with more grated cheese.

Gorgonzola Sauce

➤ NOTE: *Classically, this sauce is served with fresh fettuccine. Use a mild, creamy Gorgonzola (called dolcelatte) or a sharper, crumbly blue cheese, depending on the flavor desired.*

4	ounces Gorgonzola cheese, crumbled
½	cup milk
2	tablespoons unsalted butter
¼	cup heavy cream
	Salt
⅓	cup grated Parmesan cheese, plus more for table

▪▪ INSTRUCTIONS:

1. Place Gorgonzola, milk, and butter over medium-low heat in sauté pan large enough to hold cooked pasta. Cook, stirring often, until cheese has melted and sauce is smooth, about 4 minutes.

2. Add cream and raise heat to medium. Simmer until sauce thickens a bit, about 2 minutes. Add salt to taste.

3. Add cooked, drained pasta to cream sauce, tossing to coat noodles. Add grated cheese and continue tossing until pasta is nicely coated, about 30 seconds. Adjust seasonings and serve immediately with more grated cheese.

Porcini Mushroom Sauce
with Cream

➤ **NOTE**: *If you like, toss this intense sauce with fettuccine, preferably fresh, and ½ cup grated Parmesan cheese. Pass extra cheese at the table.*

2   ounces dried porcini mushrooms
3   tablespoons unsalted butter
1   medium onion, minced
    Salt and ground black pepper
6   tablespoons heavy cream
3   tablespoons minced fresh parsley leaves

INSTRUCTIONS:

1. Place mushrooms in small bowl. Add 2 cups hot tap water and soak until tender, about 20 minutes. Carefully lift mushrooms from liquid (*see* figure 39) and pick through to remove any foreign debris. Wash mushrooms under cold water if gritty, then chop. Strain soaking liquid through sieve lined with paper towel (*see* figure 40). Reserve mushrooms and soaking liquid separately.

2. Heat butter in large sauté pan over medium heat. Add onion and sauté until edges begin to brown, about 7 minutes. Add porcini and salt and pepper to taste and sauté to release flavors, 1 to 2 minutes.

3. Increase heat to medium-high. Add mushroom soaking liquid and simmer briskly until liquid has reduced by half, about 10 minutes. Stir in cream and simmer until sauce just starts to thicken, about 2 minutes. Stir in parsley and adjust seasonings.

Figure 39.
When soaking porcini, most of the sand and dirt will fall to the bottom of the bowl. Use a fork to lift the rehydrated mushrooms from the liquid without stirring up the sand.

Figure 40.
The soaking liquid is quite flavorful and should be reserved. To
remove grit, pour the liquid through a small sieve lined with a
single sheet of paper towel and placed over a measuring cup.

Ricotta and Parmesan Sauce with Peas

➤ **NOTE:** *Ricotta creates a rich, creamy sauce with much less fat than other dairy products. Serve with orecchiette or farfalle, which will trap the peas.*

1	10-ounce package frozen peas
	Salt
2	tablespoons olive oil
1	medium onion, minced
1	cup ricotta cheese
⅓	cup grated Parmesan cheese
2	tablespoons unsalted butter, diced
	Ground black pepper
2	tablespoons minced fresh parsley leaves (optional)

:: INSTRUCTIONS:

1. Bring water to boil in small saucepan. Add peas and salt to taste. Simmer just until almost tender, about 1 minute. Drain and reserve.

2. Heat oil in medium skillet over medium heat. Add onion and sauté until golden, about 7 minutes. Stir in peas and cook just until well-coated with oil and onions, about 1 minute. Season with salt and pepper to taste. Stir in parsley if using.

3. Stir cheeses and butter together in bowl large enough to hold cooked pasta. Stir in pea-onion mixture; adjust seasonings. Reserve ¼ cup pasta cooking water and use as needed to moisten sauce.

▦ VARIATION:

Ricotta and Parmesan Sauce with Peas and Bacon

Omit oil and cook 4 ounces (6 slices) bacon in medium skillet over medium heat until crisp, about 7 minutes. Transfer bacon to paper towel–lined plate and pour off all but 2 tablespoons fat from pan. Cook onion in bacon fat. Omit butter. Proceed with recipe, adding crumbled bacon to cheeses along with pea-onion mixture.

index